MASTERING QB64

A Comprehensive Collection of BASIC Programming Sample Codes

Olanrewaju Sanni

This book is dedicated to my lover, Lord Jesus Christ.

CONTENTS

INTRODUCTION

Welcome to Mastering QB64: A Comprehensive Collection of BASIC Programming Sample Codes. This book is designed for anyone who wants to learn how to program in QB64, a modern version of Microsoft's QuickBasic from the 1980's and 1990's. Whether you are a beginner or an experienced programmer, this book will teach you the fundamentals and advanced features of QB64, as well as how to create graphical user interfaces (GUIs) and games with it.

QB64 is a free, open-source, and cross-platform compiler that can run on Windows, Linux, Mac OS, and Android. It is compatible with most QBasic and QuickBASIC code, which means you can use it to run and modify old programs written in those languages. It also offers a number of extensions, such as OpenGL, multimedia and graphical user interface tools, that allow you to create modern applications with QB64.

This book is divided into six main chapters, each covering a different aspect of QB64 programming. In each chapter, you will find clear explanations, examples, and exercises to help you master the topic. You will also find a collection of sample codes that demonstrate how to use various QB64 features and libraries. By the end of this book, you will have a solid understanding of QB64 and be able to create your own programs with it.

The following is a brief overview of what each chapter covers:

- Chapter 1: Basic Concepts. This chapter introduces you to the basics of QB64, such as data types, variables, operators, expressions, assignments, control structures, loops, subroutines, arrays, strings, and files. You will learn how to write, compile, and run your first QB64 program, as well as how to use the QB64 IDE and debugger.

- Chapter 2: Graphics and Sound. This chapter shows you how to create graphics and sound with QB64, using the built-in screen modes, drawing commands, image and sound loading functions, and the _SND and _MAP libraries. You will learn how to draw shapes, colors, and text, display images, play and record sounds, and use the keyboard and mouse for input.

- Chapter 3: Advanced Topics. This chapter covers some of the more advanced topics of QB64, such as user-defined types and structures, pointers and memory management, error handling and debugging, external libraries and DLLs, and interfacing with C and C++. You will learn how to create and manipulate complex data structures, access and modify memory directly, handle and prevent errors, use third-party libraries and functions, and call and write C and C++ code from QB64.

- Chapter 4: GUI Development. This chapter teaches you how to create GUIs with QB64, using the InForm library. InForm is a powerful and easy-to-use tool that allows you to create windows and dialogs with various controls and widgets, such as buttons, labels, text boxes, list boxes, combo boxes, check boxes, radio buttons, sliders, progress bars, and more. You will learn how to use InForm to design and code your GUI, handle events and user input, create menus, toolbars, and status bars, and customize the look and feel of your GUI.

- Chapter 5: Game Development. This chapter guides you through the process of creating games with QB64, using the GX library. GX is a high-level and high-performance library that provides 2D and 3D graphics, sound, and input capabilities for game development. You will learn how to use GX to create sprites, animations, collisions, 3D models, lighting, cameras, sound effects, music, and more. You will also learn how to deploy your game to the web with QBjs, a tool that converts QB64 code to JavaScript and HTML5.

- Chapter 6: Appendix. This chapter contains useful reference material for QB64 programming, such as a list of QB64 keywords and functions, a list of QB64 metacommands and compiler options, a list of QB64 differences and incompatibilities with QBasic and QuickBASIC, and a list of QB64 resources and community links.

We hope you enjoy reading this book and learning QB64.

Lorem ipsum dolor sit amet, consectetur adipiscing elit, sed do eiusmod tempor incididunt ut labore et dolore magna aliqua. Ut enim ad minim veniam, quis nostrud exercitation ullamco laboris.

CHAPTER 1: BASIC CONCEPTS

This chapter introduces you to the basics of QB64, a modern version of the classic BASIC programming language. QB64 is compatible with most QBasic and QuickBasic code, but also adds new features and capabilities. You will learn how to write, compile, and run your first QB64 program, as well as how to use the QB64 integrated development environment (IDE) and debugger.

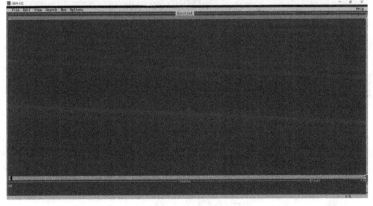

Data Types

A data type is a category of values that a variable can store. QB64 supports several data types, such as numeric, string, boolean, and user-defined types. Each data type has a specific range of values and a set of operations that can be performed on it. For example, a numeric data type can store numbers, such as integers or decimals, and can be used for arithmetic operations, such as addition or multiplication. A string data type can store text, such as words or sentences, and can be used for string manipulation, such as concatenation or extraction.

The following table summarizes the main data types in QB64 and their characteristics:

Data Type	Description	Range	Example
INTEGER	A whole number	-32768 to 32767	DIM x AS INTEGER
LONG	A large whole number	-2147483648 to 2147483647	DIM y AS LONG
SINGLE	A decimal number with single precision	-3.402823E38 to -1.401298E-45 for negative values, 1.401298E-45 to 3.402823E38 for positive values	DIM z AS SINGLE
DOUBLE	A decimal number with double precision	-1.79769313486232E308 to -4.94065645841247E-324 for negative values, 4.94065645841247E-324 to 1.79769313486232E308 for positive values	DIM w AS DOUBLE

STRING	A sequence of characters	Up to 2 billion characters	DIM s AS STRING
BOOLEAN	A logical value	TRUE or FALSE	DIM b AS BOOLEAN

Variables

A variable is a named memory location that can store a value of a certain data type. You can use variables to store data that you need for your program, such as user input, calculation results, or text messages. To use a variable, you need to declare it first, then assign a value to it, and then use it in your program.

To declare a variable, you need to use the `DIM` statement, followed by the variable name and the data type. For example, the following statement declares a variable named `age` of type `INTEGER`:

```basic
DIM age AS INTEGER
```

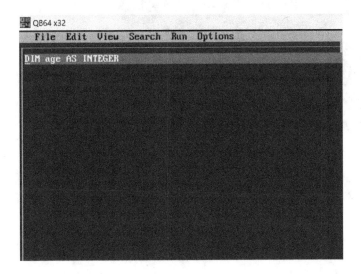

To assign a value to a variable, you need to use the ` = ` operator, followed by the value or expression. For example, the following statement assigns the value ` 10 ` to the variable ` age `:

```basic
age = 10
```

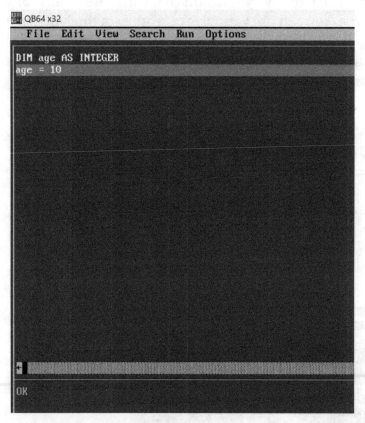

To use a variable in your program, you need to refer to it by its name. For example, the following statement prints the value of the variable ` age ` to the screen:

```basic
```

PRINT age

` ` `

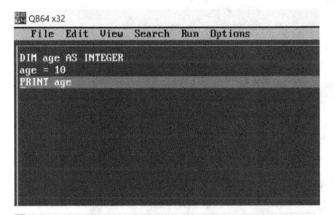

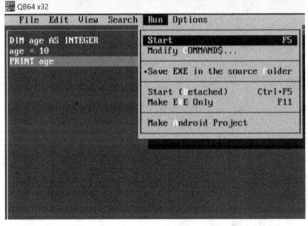

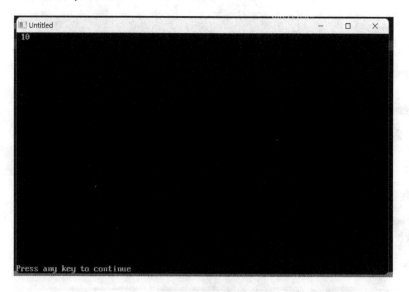

Operators And Expressions

An operator is a symbol that performs a specific operation on one or more values, called operands. For example, the `+` operator performs the addition operation on two operands, such as `2 + 3`. An expression is a combination of operators and operands that evaluates to a single value. For example, `2 + 3 * 4` is an expression that evaluates to `14`.

QB64 supports several types of operators, such as arithmetic, relational, logical, and bitwise operators. Each operator has a specific precedence and associativity, which determine the order of evaluation of the expression. For example, the `*` operator has a higher precedence than the `+` operator, which means that it is evaluated first. The following table summarizes the main operators in QB64 and their characteristics:

Operator	Description	Example	Result
+	Addition	2 + 3	5
-	Subtraction	5 – 2	3

*	Multiplication	2 * 3	6
/	Division	6 / 2	3
\	Integer division	7 \ 2	3
MOD	Modulus (remainder)	7 MOD 2	1
^	Exponentiation	2 ^ 3	8
=	Equal to	2 = 3	FALSE
<>	Not equal to	2 <> 3	TRUE
<	Less than	2 < 3	TRUE
>	Greater than	2 > 3	FALSE
<=	Less than or equal to	2 <= 3	TRUE
>=	Greater than or equal to	2 >= 3	FALSE
AND	Logical and	TRUE AND FALSE	FALSE
OR	Logical or	TRUE OR FALSE	TRUE
NOT	Logical not	NOT TRUE	FALSE
XOR	Logical exclusive or	TRUE XOR FALSE	TRUE
IMP	Logical implication	TRUE IMP FALSE	FALSE
EQV	Logical equivalence	TRUE EQV FALSE	FALSE
&	Bitwise and	5 & 3	1
		Bitwise or	5	3	7

~` || `| `` |	Bitwise not	~5	-6
<<	Bitwise left shift	5 << 1	10
>>	Bitwise right shift	5 >> 1	2

Assignments

An assignment is a statement that assigns a value or expression to a variable or a constant. You can use assignments to change the value of a variable or a constant during the execution of your program. For example, the following statement assigns the value `10` to the variable `x`:

```basic
x = 10
```

You can also use compound assignments, which combine an operator and an assignment in one statement. For example, the following statement adds `5` to the variable `x` and assigns the result back to `x`:

```basic
x += 5
```

The following table summarizes the main compound assignments in QB64 and their equivalent statements:

Compound Assignment	Equivalent Statement

x += y	x = x + y
x -= y	x = x - y
x *= y	x = x * y
x /= y	x = x / y
x \= y	x = x \ y
x MOD= y	x = x MOD y
x ^= y	x = x ^ y
x &= y	x = x & y
x |= y	x = x | y
x <<= y	x = x << y
x >>= y	x = x >> y

Control Structures

A control structure is a statement that controls the flow of execution of your program. You can use control structures to make decisions, repeat actions, or jump to different parts of your program. QB64 supports several types of control structures, such as conditional, loop, and branch statements.

Conditional Statements

A conditional statement is a statement that executes a block of code based on a condition. You can use conditional statements to perform different actions depending on the value of a variable, the result of an expression, or the input from the user. QB64 supports two types of conditional statements: `IF...THEN...ELSE` and `SELECT CASE`.

IF...THEN...ELSE

The `IF...THEN...ELSE` statement is a statement that executes one block of code if a condition is true, and another block of code if the condition is false. You can use the `IF...THEN...ELSE` statement to perform a simple binary choice in your program. For example, the following statement prints a message based on the value of the variable `score`:

```basic
IF score >= 50 THEN

    PRINT "You passed the exam!"

ELSE

    PRINT "You failed the exam!"

END IF
```

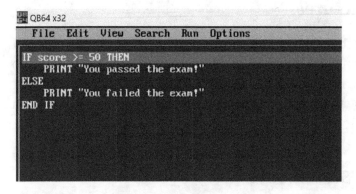

You can also use the `ELSEIF` clause to add more conditions and blocks of code to the `IF...THEN...ELSE` statement. For example, the following statement prints a message based on the value of the variable `grade`:

```basic
IF grade = "A" THEN
```

PRINT "Excellent!"

ELSEIF grade = "B" THEN

    PRINT "Good!"

ELSEIF grade = "C" THEN

    PRINT "Average!"

ELSEIF grade = "D" THEN

    PRINT "Poor!"

ELSE

    PRINT "Invalid grade!"

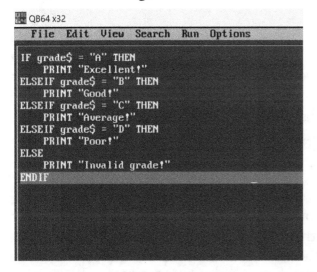

CHAPTER 2: GRAPHICS AND SOUND

In this chapter, you will learn how to create graphics and sound with QB64, using the built-in screen modes, drawing commands, image and sound loading functions, and the _SND and _MAP libraries. You will learn how to draw shapes, colors, and text, display images, play and record sounds, and use the keyboard and mouse for input.

Screen Modes

QB64 supports various screen modes, which determine the resolution, color depth, and aspect ratio of the graphics window. You can use the `SCREEN` command to set the screen mode before drawing anything. For example, `SCREEN 12` sets the screen mode to 640x480 pixels with 16 colors, while `SCREEN 13` sets the screen mode to 320x200 pixels with 256 colors. You can also use `SCREEN 0` to set the screen mode to the default text mode, or `SCREEN _NEWIMAGE(width, height, bits)` to create a custom screen mode with the specified width, height, and color depth. For example, `SCREEN _NEWIMAGE(800, 600, 32)` creates a screen mode with 800x600 pixels and 32-bit colors.

To get the current screen mode, you can use the `_MODE`

function, which returns a numerical value corresponding to the screen mode. You can also use the `_WIDTH` and `_HEIGHT` functions to get the width and height of the graphics window, and the `_PIXELSIZE` function to get the size of a pixel in bytes.

Here is an example program that displays the current screen mode and some basic information:

```basic
SCREEN 13 'set screen mode to 320x200 with 256 colors
CLS 'clear the screen
PRINT "Screen mode: "; _MODE 'print the screen mode
PRINT "Width: "; _WIDTH 'print the width
PRINT "Height: "; _HEIGHT 'print the height
PRINT "Pixel size: "; _PIXELSIZE 'print the pixel size
SLEEP 'wait for a key press
```

Drawing Commands

QB64 provides several commands for drawing graphics on the screen, such as `PSET`, `LINE`, `CIRCLE`, `PAINT`, and `DRAW`. You can use these commands to draw pixels, lines, circles, ellipses, rectangles, polygons, and other shapes. You can also use the `COLOR` command to set the foreground and background colors, and the `_RGB` function to create custom colors from red, green, and blue values.

Here is an example program that draws a rainbow using the `CIRCLE` and `COLOR` commands:

```basic
SCREEN 13 'set screen mode to 320x200 with 256 colors
CLS 'clear the screen
FOR i = 1 TO 7 'loop from 1 to 7
    COLOR i 'set the color to i
    CIRCLE (160, 100), 100 - i * 10, , , 0.5 'draw a circle with the
center at (160, 100), the radius at 100 - i * 10, and the aspect ratio
at 0.5
NEXT i 'next iteration
SLEEP 'wait for a key press
```

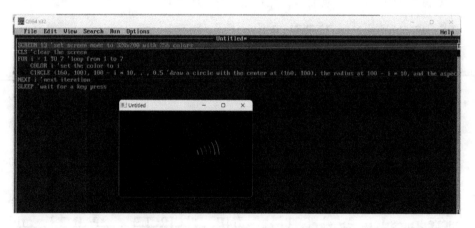

Image And Sound Loading Functions

QB64 allows you to load and display images and sounds from external files, using the `_LOADIMAGE` and `_SNDOPEN` functions. You can use the `_LOADIMAGE` function to load an image file (such as BMP, PNG, JPG, or GIF) and return a handle to the image. You can then use the `_PUTIMAGE` command to display the image on the screen, specifying the coordinates and the optional scaling factor. You can also use the `_FREEIMAGE` command to free the memory used by the image when you are done with it.

You can use the `_SNDOPEN` function to load a sound file (such as WAV, MP3, OGG, or MIDI) and return a handle to the sound. You can then use the `_SNDPLAY` command to play the sound, specifying the handle and the optional looping flag. You can also use the `_SNDSTOP` command to stop the sound, and the `_SNDCLOSE` command to close the sound and free the memory.

Here is an example program that loads and displays an image and plays a sound:

```basic
SCREEN 13 'set screen mode to 320x200 with 256 colors

CLS 'clear the screen

image = _LOADIMAGE("logo.bmp") 'load the image file

_PUTIMAGE (0, 0), image 'display the image at (0, 0)

_FREEIMAGE image 'free the image

sound = _SNDOPEN("music.mp3") 'load the sound file

_SNDPLAY sound, 1 'play the sound with looping

SLEEP 'wait for a key press

_SNDSTOP sound 'stop the sound

_SNDCLOSE sound 'close the sound
```

The _Snd And _Map Libraries

QB64 also provides two libraries for advanced sound and graphics manipulation: the _SND and _MAP libraries. The _SND library allows you to create, modify, and mix sounds in memory, using commands such as `_SNDNEW`, `_SNDLEN`, `_SNDCOPY`, `_SNDMODULATE`, and `_SNDVOL`. The _MAP library allows you to create, modify, and display images in memory, using commands such as `_MAPNEW`, `_MAPTRI`, `_MAPTEXTURE`, `_MAPCOLOR`, and `_MAPSHOW`.

Here is an example program that uses the _SND library to create a simple synthesizer:

```basic
SCREEN 0 'set screen mode to text mode

CLS 'clear the screen

PRINT "Press keys A to K to play notes, Q to quit" 'print instructions

DO 'start a loop

    k$ = INKEY$ 'get a key press

    IF k$ <> "" THEN 'if a key was pressed

        SELECT CASE k$ 'select the case based on the key

            CASE "a" 'if the key was a

                f = 261.63 'set the frequency to C4

            CASE "s" 'if the key was s

                f = 293.66 'set the frequency to D4

            CASE "d" 'if the key was d

                f = 329.63 'set the frequency to E4

            CASE "f" 'if the key was f

                f = 349.23 'set the frequency to F4

            CASE "g" 'if the key was g

                f = 392 'set the frequency to G4
```

```
CASE "h" 'if the key was h
    f = 440 'set the frequency to A4
CASE "j" 'if the key was j
    f = 493.88 'set the frequency to B4
CASE "k" 'if the key was k
    f = 523.25 'set the frequency to C5
CASE "q" 'if the key was q
    EXIT DO 'exit the loop
CASE ELSE 'if the key was anything else
    f = 0 'set the frequency to 0
END SELECT 'end the select
IF f > 0 THEN 'if the frequency is positive
    s = _SNDNEW(1, f * 2, 16, 1) 'create a new sound with 1
second, f * 2 samples, 16 bits, and 1 channel
    FOR i = 0 TO f * 2 - 1 'loop from 0 to f * 2 - 1
        v = 32767 * SIN(i * _PI(2) / f) 'calculate the sine wave
value
        _SNDCOPY s, i, v 'copy the value to the sound
    NEXT i 'next iteration
    _SNDPLAY s 'play the sound
    _SNDFREE s 'free the sound
END IF 'end the if
END IF 'end the if
LOOP 'end the loop
```

```

```

Here is an example program that uses the _MAP library to create a simple animation:

```basic
SCREEN 13 'set screen mode to 320x200 with 256 colors
CLS 'clear the screen
m = _MAPNEW(100, 100) 'create a new map with 100x100 pixels
FOR i = 1 TO 255 'loop from 1 to 255
    _MAPCOLOR m, i 'set the map color to i
    _MAPTRI m, 50, 0, 0, 100, 100, 100 'draw a triangle on the map
    _MAPSHOW m, 110, 50 'show the map at (110, 50)
    _MAPCOLOR m, 0 'set the map color to 0
    _MAPTRI m, 50, 0, 0, 100, 100, 100 'erase the triangle on the map
NEXT i 'next iteration
_MAPFREE m 'free the map
SLEEP 'wait for a key press
```

Keyboard And Mouse Input

QB64 also provides several commands and functions for getting keyboard and mouse input, such as `INKEY$`, `KEY`, `_KEYHIT`, `_MOUSEINPUT`, `_MOUSEX`, `_MOUSEY`, and `_MOUSEBUTTON`. You can use these commands and functions to detect key presses, key states, mouse movements, and mouse clicks.

Here is an example

```basic
SCREEN 13 'set screen mode to 320x200 with 256 colors
CLS 'clear the screen
x = 160 'set the initial x coordinate
y = 100 'set the initial y coordinate
DO 'start a loop
    _MOUSEINPUT 'get the mouse input
    mx = _MOUSEX 'get the mouse x coordinate
    my = _MOUSEY 'get the mouse y coordinate
    mb = _MOUSEBUTTON(1) 'get the mouse left button state
    IF mb THEN 'if the mouse left button is pressed
        LINE (x, y)-(mx, my), 15 'draw a line from (x, y) to (mx, my) with color 15
        x = mx 'update the x coordinate
        y = my 'update the y coordinate
    END IF 'end the if
    k = _KEYHIT 'get a key press
    IF k = 27 THEN 'if the key is ESC
        EXIT DO 'exit the loop
    END IF 'end the if
LOOP 'end the loop
```

This program allows you to draw lines on the screen with the mouse, and quit with the ESC key. I hope you enjoyed this chapter on graphics and sound with QB64.

CHAPTER 3:
ADVANCED TOPICS

I n this chapter, you will learn some of the more advanced topics of QB64, such as user-defined types and structures, pointers and memory management, error handling and debugging, external libraries and DLLs, and interfacing with C and C++. You will learn how to create and manipulate complex data structures, access and modify memory directly, handle and prevent errors, use third-party libraries and functions, and call and write C and C++ code from QB64.

User-Defined Types And Structures

QB64 allows you to define your own data types and structures, using the `TYPE` and `END TYPE` keywords. You can use these keywords to create a new type with multiple fields of different data types, such as integers, strings, arrays, or other user-defined types. You can then use the `DIM` command to declare variables of the new type, and use the dot operator (`.`) to access the fields of the variables.

Here is an example program that defines a new type called `Person`, which has three fields: `name`, `age`, and `gender`. The program then declares an array of 10 `Person` variables, and assigns some values to them. The program then prints the name and age of each person in the array.

```basic
TYPE Person 'define a new type called Person

    name AS STRING 'declare a field called name of type STRING

    age AS INTEGER 'declare a field called age of type INTEGER

    gender AS STRING 'declare a field called gender of type STRING

END TYPE 'end the type definition

DIM people(1 TO 10) AS Person 'declare an array of 10 Person variables

people(1).name = "Alice" 'assign the name of the first person to "Alice"

people(1).age = 25 'assign the age of the first person to 25

people(1).gender = "F" 'assign the gender of the first person to "F"

people(2).name = "Bob" 'assign the name of the second person to "Bob"

people(2).age = 30 'assign the age of the second person to 30

people(2).gender = "M" 'assign the gender of the second person to "M"

'... assign values to the rest of the people

FOR i = 1 TO 10 'loop from 1 to 10

    PRINT people(i).name; " is "; people(i).age; " years old." 'print the name and age of each person

NEXT i 'next iteration
```

Pointers And Memory Management

QB64 also allows you to use pointers and memory management, using the `` `_MEM` `` and `` `_OFFSET` `` functions, and the `` `VARPTR` ``, `` `PEEK` ``, and `` `POKE` `` commands. You can use these functions and commands to get the address of a variable or a memory block, read or write bytes from a memory location, and allocate or free memory dynamically.

Here is an example program that uses pointers and memory management to create a linked list of integers. The program uses the `` `_MEM` `` function to allocate memory for each node of the list, and the `` `_OFFSET` `` function to get the address of the next node. The program uses the `` `VARPTR` ``, `` `PEEK` ``, and `` `POKE` `` commands to store and retrieve the data and the pointer of each node. The program then prints the values of the list, and frees the memory of each node.

```basic
CONST SIZEOF_INT = 4 'define the size of an integer in bytes
CONST SIZEOF_PTR = 8 'define the size of a pointer in bytes
DIM head AS LONG 'declare a variable to store the head of the list
DIM current AS LONG 'declare a variable to store the current node of the list
DIM data AS INTEGER 'declare a variable to store the data of each node
DIM next AS LONG 'declare a variable to store the pointer of each node
head = _MEM(SIZEOF_INT + SIZEOF_PTR) 'allocate memory for the first node
current = head 'set the current node to the head
data = 10 'set the data to 10
POKE current, data 'store the data in the current node
```

next = _MEM(SIZEOF_INT + SIZEOF_PTR) 'allocate memory for the next node

POKE current + SIZEOF_INT, next 'store the pointer to the next node in the current node

current = next 'set the current node to the next node

data = 20 'set the data to 20

POKE current, data 'store the data in the current node

next = _MEM(SIZEOF_INT + SIZEOF_PTR) 'allocate memory for the next node

POKE current + SIZEOF_INT, next 'store the pointer to the next node in the current node

current = next 'set the current node to the next node

data = 30 'set the data to 30

POKE current, data 'store the data in the current node

next = 0 'set the pointer to 0

POKE current + SIZEOF_INT, next 'store the pointer to 0 in the current node

current = head 'set the current node to the head

DO 'start a loop

    data = PEEK(current) 'retrieve the data from the current node

    PRINT data 'print the data

    next = PEEK(current + SIZEOF_INT) 'retrieve the pointer from the current node

    IF next = 0 THEN 'if the pointer is 0

        EXIT DO 'exit the loop

    END IF 'end the if

    current = next 'set the current node to the next node

LOOP 'end the loop

current = head 'set the current node to the head

DO 'start a loop

    next = PEEK(current + SIZEOF_INT) 'retrieve the pointer from the current node

    _MEMFREE current 'free the memory of the current node

    IF next = 0 THEN 'if the pointer is 0

      EXIT DO 'exit the loop

    END IF 'end the if

    current = next 'set the current node to the next node

LOOP 'end the loop

` ` `

Error Handling And Debugging

QB64 also provides some commands and functions for error handling and debugging, such as `ON ERROR`, `RESUME`, `ERR`, `ERL`, and `_ERRORLINE`. You can use these commands and functions to catch and handle runtime errors, resume the program execution, get the error number and description, and get the line number and source code of the error.

Here is an example program that uses error handling and debugging to catch and handle a division by zero error. The program uses the `ON ERROR` command to set a label for the error handler, and the `RESUME` command to resume the program execution after handling the error. The program uses the `ERR` and `ERL` functions to get the error number and line number, and the `_ERRORLINE` function to get the source code of the error.

```basic
ON ERROR GOTO ErrorHandler 'set the error handler label
DIM a AS INTEGER 'declare a variable to store the dividend
DIM b AS INTEGER 'declare a variable to store the divisor
DIM c AS INTEGER 'declare a variable to store the quotient
a = 10 'set the dividend to 10
b = 0 'set the divisor to 0
c = a / b 'try to divide by zero
PRINT "The quotient is "; c 'print the quotient
END 'end the program
ErrorHandler: 'the error handler label
PRINT "An error occurred: "; ERR; " - "; _ERRORLINE(ERL) 'print the error number and source code
PRINT "Please check the divisor and try again." 'print a message to the user
RESUME NEXT 'resume the program execution at the next line
```

External Libraries And Dlls

QB64 also allows you to use external libraries and DLLs, using the `DECLARE LIBRARY` and `END DECLARE` keywords, and the `ALIAS` and `BYVAL` modifiers. You can use these keywords and modifiers to declare the name and location of the library or DLL, and the name, parameters, and return type of the functions in the library or DLL. You can then use the declared functions in your program, passing the arguments by value or by reference, and getting the return value if any.

Here is an example program that uses an external library called `libcurl.dll`, which is a library for transferring data with URLs. The program uses the `DECLARE LIBRARY` and `END DECLARE` keywords to declare the name and location of the library, and the `ALIAS` and `BYVAL` modifiers to declare the name, parameters, and return type of the functions in the library. The program then uses the declared functions to initialize the library, set the URL, perform the transfer, and clean up the library.

```basic
DECLARE LIBRARY "libcurl.dll" 'declare the name and location of the library

    FUNCTION curl_easy_init ALIAS "curl_easy_init" () AS LONG 'declare the function to initialize the library

    FUNCTION curl_easy_setopt ALIAS "curl_easy_setopt" (BYVAL handle AS LONG, BYVAL option AS LONG, BYVAL parameter AS LONG) AS LONG 'declare the function to set the options

    FUNCTION curl_easy_perform ALIAS "curl_easy_perform" (BYVAL handle AS LONG) AS LONG 'declare the function to perform the transfer

    FUNCTION curl_easy_cleanup ALIAS "curl_easy_cleanup" (BYVAL handle AS LONG) 'declare the function to clean up the library

END DECLARE 'end the library declaration

CONST CURLOPT_URL = 10002 'define the option to set the URL

DIM handle AS LONG 'declare a variable to store the handle of the library

DIM url AS STRING 'declare a variable to store the URL

DIM result AS LONG 'declare a variable to store the result of the transfer

handle = curl_easy_init 'initialize the library
```

```
IF handle THEN 'if the handle is valid
    url = "https://www.qb64.org" 'set the URL to the QB64 website
    result   =   curl_easy_setopt(handle,   CURLOPT_URL,
VARPTR(url)) 'set the option to the URL
    IF result = 0 THEN 'if the option was set successfully
        result = curl_easy_perform(handle) 'perform the transfer
        IF result = 0 THEN 'if the transfer was successful
            PRINT "Transfer completed." 'print a message
        ELSE 'if the transfer failed
            PRINT "Transfer failed: "; result 'print the error code
        END IF 'end the if
    ELSE 'if the option failed
        PRINT "Option failed: "; result 'print the error code
    END IF 'end the if
    curl_easy_cleanup(handle) 'clean up the library
ELSE 'if the handle is invalid
    PRINT "Initialization failed." 'print a message
END IF 'end the if
```

C And C++ Interfacing

QB64 also allows you to interface with C and C++ code, using the `$INCLUDE` and `$INSERT` metacommands, and the `BYVAL`, `BYREF`, and `CDECL` modifiers. You can use these metacommands and modifiers to include C and C++ header files, insert C and C++ source code, and declare and call C and C++ functions from QB64.

Here is an example program that uses C and C++ interfacing to calculate the factorial of a number. The program uses the ` $INCLUDE ` metacommand to include the `math.h` header file, which contains the declaration of the `factorial` function. The program uses the ` $INSERT ` metacommand to insert the C source code that defines the `factorial` function. The program then declares the `factorial` function with the `CDECL` modifier, which indicates that it uses the C calling convention. The program then calls the `factorial` function with the `BYVAL` modifier, which indicates that it passes the argument by value. The program then prints the return value of the function.

```basic
$INCLUDE "math.h" 'include the math.h header file

$INSERT "factorial.c" 'insert the factorial.c source code

DECLARE CDECL FUNCTION factorial (BYVAL n AS LONG) AS LONG 'declare the factorial function

DIM x AS LONG 'declare a variable to store the input

DIM y AS LONG 'declare a variable to store the output

INPUT "Enter a number: ", x 'get the input from the user

y = factorial(x) 'call the factorial function

PRINT "The factorial of "; x; " is "; y 'print the output
```

This is the content of the `factorial.c` source code:

```c
long factorial(long n) { //define the factorial function
    if (n == 0 || n == 1) { //if n is 0 or 1
```

```
    return 1; //return 1
  } else { //else
    return n * factorial(n - 1); //return n times the factorial of n
- 1
  }
}
` ` `
```

CHAPTER 4: GUI DEVELOPMENT

I n this chapter, you will learn how to create GUIs with QB64, using the InForm library. InForm is a powerful and easy-to-use tool that allows you to create windows and dialogs with various controls and widgets, such as buttons, labels, text boxes, list boxes, combo boxes, check boxes, radio buttons, sliders, progress bars, and more. You will learn how to use InForm to design and code your GUI, handle events and user input, create menus, toolbars, and status bars, and customize the look and feel of your GUI.

Installing And Using Inform

To use InForm, you need to download and install the InForm library from the [QB64 website](https://www.qb64.org/portal/inform/). You also need to include the `InForm.bi` file in your program, using the `$INCLUDE` metacommand. For example:

```basic
$INCLUDE "InForm.bi" 'include the InForm library
```

To create a GUI with InForm, you need to follow these steps:

1. Create a window or a dialog, using the `Window` or `Dialog` commands. You can specify the title, size, position, style, and icon of the window or dialog. For example:

```basic
Window "My GUI", 400, 300, 100, 100, _WINDOWED 'create a window with the title "My GUI", the size 400x300, and the position 100, 100
```

2. Add controls and widgets to the window or dialog, using the `Control` command. You can specify the type, name, text, size, position, style, and events of the control or widget. For example:

```basic
Control Button, "btnOK", "OK", 100, 50, 50, 20, , , Clicked 'add a button with the name "btnOK", the text "OK", the size 50x20, and the position 100, 50
```

3. Show the window or dialog, using the `Show` command. You can specify the modal or modeless mode of the window or dialog. For example:

```basic
Show 'show the window in modeless mode
```

4. Handle the events and user input of the window or dialog, using the `Event` function and the `Select Case` statement. You can use the `Event` function to get the name of the control or widget that triggered the event, and the `Select Case` statement to perform different actions based on the event name. For example:

```basic
DO 'start a loop
    ev$ = Event 'get the event name
    SELECT CASE ev$ 'select the case based on the event name
        CASE "btnOK" 'if the event name is "btnOK"
            PRINT "You clicked OK." 'print a message
        CASE "FormClose" 'if the event name is "FormClose"
            EXIT DO 'exit the loop
    END SELECT 'end the select
LOOP 'end the loop
```

5. Close the window or dialog, using the `Close` command. You can specify the name of the window or dialog to close. For example:

```basic
Close 'close the window
```

Creating Menus, Toolbars, And Status Bars

InForm also allows you to create menus, toolbars, and status bars for your GUI, using the `Menu`, `Toolbar`, and `Statusbar` commands. You can use these commands to add items, buttons, and panels to the menu, toolbar, and status bar, and specify the text, icon, style, and events of each item, button, or panel. For example:

```basic
Menu "File", "New", "Open", "Save", "Exit" 'create a menu with the items "File", "New", "Open", "Save", and "Exit"

Toolbar "New", "Open", "Save" 'create a toolbar with the buttons "New", "Open", and "Save"

Statusbar "Ready" 'create a status bar with the panel "Ready"
```

You can handle the events and user input of the menu, toolbar, and status bar, using the same method as the controls and widgets. For example:

```basic
DO 'start a loop
    ev$ = Event 'get the event name
    SELECT CASE ev$ 'select the case based on the event name
        CASE "New" 'if the event name is "New"
            PRINT "You clicked New." 'print a message
        CASE "Open" 'if the event name is "Open"
            PRINT "You clicked Open." 'print a message
        CASE "Save" 'if the event name is "Save"
            PRINT "You clicked Save." 'print a message
        CASE "Exit" 'if the event name is "Exit"
```

```
        EXIT DO 'exit the loop
     CASE "FormClose" 'if the event name is "FormClose"
        EXIT DO 'exit the loop
   END SELECT 'end the select
LOOP 'end the loop
```
``` ` ` ` ```

Customizing The Look And Feel Of Your Gui

InForm also allows you to customize the look and feel of your GUI, using the `Theme` command and the `_RGB` function. You can use the `Theme` command to set the theme of your GUI, such as `_THEME_FLAT`, `_THEME_OFFICE`, or `_THEME_AERO`. You can also use the `_RGB` function to create custom colors from red, green, and blue values, and use them to set the background, foreground, border, and highlight colors of your GUI. For example:

``` ` ` `basic ```
```
Theme _THEME_FLAT 'set the theme to flat
BackColor _RGB(255, 255, 255) 'set the background color to white
ForeColor _RGB(0, 0, 0) 'set the foreground color to black
BorderColor _RGB(128, 128, 128) 'set the border color to gray
HighlightColor _RGB(0, 0, 255) 'set the highlight color to blue
```
``` ` ` ` ```
```

CHAPTER 5: GAME DEVELOPMENT

I n this chapter, you will learn how to create games with QB64, using the GX library. GX is a high-level and high-performance library that provides 2D and 3D graphics, sound, and input capabilities for game development. You will learn how to use GX to create sprites, animations, collisions, 3D models, lighting, cameras, sound effects, music, and more. You will also learn how to deploy your game to the web with QBjs, a tool that converts QB64 code to JavaScript and HTML5.

Installing And Using Gx

To use GX, you need to download and install the GX library from the [QB64 website](https://www.qb64.org/portal/gx/). You also need to include the `GX.bi` file in your program, using the `$INCLUDE` metacommand. For example:

```basic
$INCLUDE "GX.bi" 'include the GX library
```

To create a game with GX, you need to follow these steps:

1. Initialize the GX library, using the `GX_Init` command. You can specify the title, width, height, and flags of the game window. For example:

```basic
GX_Init "My Game", 800, 600, _GX_WINDOWED 'initialize the
GX library with the title "My Game", the size 800x600, and the
windowed mode
```

2. Load the resources for your game, such as images, sounds, fonts, and models, using the `GX_LoadImage`, `GX_LoadSound`, `GX_LoadFont`, and `GX_LoadModel` commands. You can specify the file name and the optional flags of the resource. For example:

```basic
player = GX_LoadImage("player.png") 'load the image file for the
player

enemy = GX_LoadImage("enemy.png") 'load the image file for the
enemy

bullet = GX_LoadImage("bullet.png") 'load the image file for the
bullet

explosion = GX_LoadSound("explosion.wav") 'load the sound file
for the explosion

music = GX_LoadSound("music.mp3") 'load the sound file for the
music

font = GX_LoadFont("font.ttf", 32) 'load the font file with the size
```

32

```basic
cube = GX_LoadModel("cube.obj") 'load the model file for the cube
```
```

3. Create the main loop for your game, using the `DO` and `LOOP` keywords. You can use the `GX_Exit` function to check if the user wants to quit the game, and the `GX_Flip` command to update the game screen. For example:

```basic
DO 'start the main loop

    IF GX_Exit THEN EXIT DO 'if the user wants to quit, exit the loop

    '... update the game logic and input

    '... render the game graphics and sound

    GX_Flip 'update the game screen
LOOP 'end the main loop
```
```

4. Clean up the GX library, using the `GX_Cleanup` command. You can also use the `GX_FreeImage`, `GX_FreeSound`, `GX_FreeFont`, and `GX_FreeModel` commands to free the memory used by the resources. For example:

```basic
GX_Cleanup 'clean up the GX library
GX_FreeImage player 'free the image for the player
GX_FreeImage enemy 'free the image for the enemy
```

GX_FreeImage bullet 'free the image for the bullet

GX_FreeSound explosion 'free the sound for the explosion

GX_FreeSound music 'free the sound for the music

GX_FreeFont font 'free the font

GX_FreeModel cube 'free the model

` ` `

Creating Sprites And Animations

GX allows you to create sprites and animations for your game, using the `GX_Sprite` and `GX_Animation` commands. You can use the `GX_Sprite` command to create a sprite from an image, and specify the position, rotation, scale, color, and alpha of the sprite. You can also use the `GX_Animation` command to create an animation from a sprite sheet, and specify the number of frames, the frame rate, and the looping mode of the animation. For example:

` ` `basic

playerSprite = GX_Sprite(player, 100, 100, 0, 1, 1, _RGB(255, 255, 255), 255) 'create a sprite for the player from the player image, and set the position to (100, 100), the rotation to 0, the scale to 1, the color to white, and the alpha to 255

enemySprite = GX_Sprite(enemy, 700, 100, 0, 1, 1, _RGB(255, 255, 255), 255) 'create a sprite for the enemy from the enemy image, and set the position to (700, 100), the rotation to 0, the scale to 1, the color to white, and the alpha to 255

bulletSprite = GX_Sprite(bullet, 0, 0, 0, 1, 1, _RGB(255, 255, 255), 255) 'create a sprite for the bullet from the bullet image, and set the position to (0, 0), the rotation to 0, the scale to 1, the color to white, and the alpha to 255

explosionAnimation = GX_Animation(explosion, 64, 64, 16, 10, _GX_ANIM_LOOP) 'create an animation for the explosion from the explosion image, and set the frame size to 64x64, the number of frames to 16, the frame rate to 10, and the looping mode to loop

` ` `

You can use the `GX_DrawSprite` and `GX_DrawAnimation` commands to draw the sprites and animations on the screen, and specify the optional blending mode and layer of the sprite or animation. You can also use the `GX_MoveSprite`, `GX_RotateSprite`, `GX_ScaleSprite`, `GX_ColorSprite`, and `GX_AlphaSprite` commands to modify the position, rotation, scale, color, and alpha of the sprite. For example:

```basic
GX_DrawSprite playerSprite, _GX_BLEND_ALPHA, 0 'draw the player sprite with alpha blending and layer 0

GX_DrawSprite enemySprite, _GX_BLEND_ALPHA, 0 'draw the enemy sprite with alpha blending and layer 0

GX_DrawSprite bulletSprite, _GX_BLEND_ALPHA, 0 'draw the bullet sprite with alpha blending and layer 0

GX_DrawAnimation explosionAnimation, 200, 200, _GX_BLEND_ADD, 1 'draw the explosion animation at (200, 200) with additive blending and layer 1

GX_MoveSprite playerSprite, 100 + SIN(TIMER) * 50, 100 'move the player sprite horizontally with a sine wave

GX_RotateSprite enemySprite, enemySprite.angle + 1 'rotate the enemy sprite by 1 degree

GX_ScaleSprite bulletSprite, bulletSprite.scaleX + 0.01, bulletSprite.scaleY + 0.01 'scale the bullet sprite by 0.01

GX_ColorSprite playerSprite, _RGB(255, 0, 0) 'change the color of
```

the player sprite to red

GX_AlphaSprite enemySprite, enemySprite.alpha - 1 'decrease the alpha of the enemy sprite by 1

` ` `

Creating Collisions

GX allows you to create collisions for your game, using the `GX_Collision` command. You can use the `GX_Collision` command to check if two sprites or animations are colliding, and get the collision point and normal. You can also use the `GX_BoundingBox` and `GX_BoundingCircle` commands to get the bounding box and bounding circle of a sprite or animation, and use them for collision detection. For example:

```basic
IF GX_Collision(playerSprite, enemySprite) THEN 'if the player sprite and the enemy sprite are colliding
    PRINT "Game over!" 'print a message
    EXIT DO 'exit the loop
END IF 'end the if
IF GX_Collision(bulletSprite, enemySprite) THEN 'if the bullet sprite and the enemy sprite are colliding
    PRINT "You hit the enemy!" 'print a message
    GX_PlaySound explosion 'play the explosion sound
    GX_FreeSprite bulletSprite 'free the bullet sprite
    GX_FreeSprite enemySprite 'free the enemy sprite
END IF 'end the if
playerBox = GX_BoundingBox(playerSprite) 'get the bounding box
```

of the player sprite

enemyBox = GX_BoundingBox(enemySprite) 'get the bounding box of the enemy sprite

bulletCircle = GX_BoundingCircle(bulletSprite) 'get the bounding circle of the bullet sprite

enemyCircle = GX_BoundingCircle(enemySprite) 'get the bounding circle of the enemy sprite

IF GX_Collision(playerBox, enemyBox) THEN 'if the player box and the enemy box are colliding

    PRINT "Game over!" 'print a message

    EXIT DO 'exit the loop

END IF 'end the if

IF GX_Collision(bulletCircle, enemyCircle) THEN 'if the bullet circle and the enemy circle are colliding

    PRINT "You hit the enemy!" 'print a message

    GX_PlaySound explosion 'play the explosion sound

    GX_FreeSprite bulletSprite 'free the bullet sprite

    GX_FreeSprite enemySprite 'free the enemy sprite

END IF 'end the if

` ` `

Creating 3D Models, Lighting, And Cameras

GX allows you to create 3D models, lighting, and cameras for your game, using the `GX_Model`, `GX_Light`, and `GX_Camera` commands. You can use the `GX_Model` command to create a 3D model from a file or a primitive shape, and specify the position, rotation, scale, color, and texture of the model. You can also use the `GX_Light` command to create a light source, and specify the type, position, direction, color, and intensity of the light. You can also use the `GX_Camera` command to create a camera, and specify the position, target, up vector, field of view, and clipping planes of the camera. For example:

```basic
cube = GX_Model(cube, 0, 0, 0, 0, 0, 0, 1, 1, 1, _RGB(255, 255, 255), 0) 'create a model for the cube from the cube file, and set the position to (0, 0, 0), the rotation to (0, 0, 0), the scale to (1, 1, 1), the color to white, and the texture to 0

sphere = GX_Model(_GX_SPHERE, 0, 0, 0, 0, 0, 0, 1, 1, 1, _RGB(255, 0, 0), 0) 'create a model for the sphere from the sphere primitive, and set the position to (0, 0, 0), the rotation to (0, 0, 0), the scale to (1, 1, 1), the color to red, and the texture to 0

light = GX_Light(_GX_POINT, 0, 0, 0, 0, 0, 0, _RGB(255, 255, 255), 1) 'create a light source of type point, and set the position to (0, 0, 0), the direction to (0, 0, 0), the color to white, and the intensity to 1

camera = GX_Camera(0, 0, 10, 0, 0, 0, 0, 1, 0, 60, 0.1, 100) 'create a camera, and set the position to (0, 0, 10), the target to (0, 0, 0), the up vector to (0, 1, 0), the field of view to 60, and the clipping planes to 0.1 and 100
```

You can use the `GX_DrawModel` command to draw the 3D models on the screen, and specify the optional blending mode and layer of the model. You can also use the `GX_MoveModel`, `GX_RotateModel`, `GX_ScaleModel`, `GX_ColorModel`, and `GX_TextureModel` commands to modify the position, rotation, scale, color, and texture of the model. For example:

```basic
GX_DrawModel cube, _GX_BLEND_ALPHA, 0 'draw the cube
```

model with alpha blending and layer 0

GX_DrawModel sphere, _GX_BLEND_ALPHA, 0 'draw the sphere model with alpha blending and layer 0

GX_MoveModel cube, 0 + COS(TIMER) * 5, 0, 0 'move the cube model horizontally with a cosine wave

GX_RotateModel sphere, sphere.angleX + 1, sphere.angleY + 1, sphere.angleZ + 1 'rotate the sphere model by 1 degree on each axis

GX_ScaleModel cube, cube.scaleX + 0.01, cube.scaleY + 0.01, cube.scaleZ + 0.01 'scale the cube model by 0.01 on each axis

GX_ColorModel sphere, _RGB(0, 255, 0) 'change the color of the sphere model to green

GX_TextureModel cube, 1 'change the texture of the cube model to 1

` ` `

You can use the `GX_MoveLight`, `GX_DirLight`, `GX_ColorLight`, and `GX_IntensityLight` commands to modify the position, direction, color, and intensity of the light source. You can also use the `GX_MoveCamera`, `GX_TargetCamera`, `GX_UpCamera`, `GX_FovCamera`, and `GX_ClipCamera` commands to modify the position, target, up vector, field of view, and clipping planes of the camera. For example:

` ` `basic

GX_MoveLight light, 0 + SIN(TIMER) * 10, 0 + COS(TIMER) * 10, 0 'move the light source in a circular path

GX_DirLight light, -light.x, -light.y, -light.z 'set the direction of the light source to the opposite of its position

GX_ColorLight light, _RGB(255, 255, 0) 'change the color of the light source to yellow

GX_IntensityLight light, 1 + SIN(TIMER) * 0.5 'change the intensity of the light source with a sine wave

GX_MoveCamera camera, 0, 0, 10 + SIN(TIMER) * 5 'move the camera back and forth with a sine wave

GX_TargetCamera camera, 0, 0, 0 'set the target of the camera to the origin

GX_UpCamera camera, 0, 1, 0 'set the up vector of the camera to the y-axis

GX_FovCamera camera, 60 + COS(TIMER) * 10 'change the field of view of the camera with a cosine wave

GX_ClipCamera camera, 0.1, 100 'set the clipping planes of the camera to 0.1 and 100

` ` `

CHAPTER 6: APPENDIX

This chapter contains useful reference material for QB64 programming, such as a list of QB64 keywords and functions, a list of QB64 metacommands and compiler options, a list of QB64 differences and incompatibilities with QBasic and QuickBASIC, and a list of QB64 resources and community links.

Qb64 Keywords And Functions

QB64 supports most of the keywords and functions of QBasic and QuickBASIC, as well as some new ones that extend the functionality and compatibility of the language. Here is a list of some of the most common and useful QB64 keywords and functions, grouped by category:

- Arithmetic and Math:

`+`, `-`, `*`, `/`, `\`, `^`, `MOD`, `ABS`, `ATN`, `COS`, `EXP`, `INT`, `LOG`, `RND`, `SIN`, `SQR`, `TAN`, etc.

- Assignment and Comparison:

`=`, `<>`, `<`, `>`, `<=`, `>=`, `AND`, `OR`, `NOT`, `XOR`,

`EQV`, `IMP`, etc.

- Control Flow and Looping:

`IF`, `THEN`, `ELSE`, `ELSEIF`, `END IF`, `SELECT CASE`, `CASE`, `CASE ELSE`, `END SELECT`, `FOR`, `TO`, `STEP`, `NEXT`, `WHILE`, `WEND`, `DO`, `LOOP`, `UNTIL`, `EXIT`, `GOTO`, `GOSUB`, `RETURN`, etc.

- Data Types and Conversion:

`INTEGER`, `LONG`, `SINGLE`, `DOUBLE`, `STRING`, `FIXED`, `_BYTE`, `_INTEGER64`, `_FLOAT`, `_UNSIGNED`, `TYPE`, `END TYPE`, `DIM`, `REDIM`, `SHARED`, `COMMON`, `DATA`, `READ`, `RESTORE`, `CINT`, `CLNG`, `CSNG`, `CDBL`, `CSTR`, `CVAR`, `MKI$`, `MKL$`, `MKS$`, `MKD$`, `CVI`, `CVL`, `CVS`, `CVD`, etc.

- File and Console Input/Output:

`OPEN`, `CLOSE`, `INPUT`, `LINE INPUT`, `PRINT`, `WRITE`, `READ`, `LOC`, `LOF`, `EOF`, `SEEK`, `FIELD`, `GET`, `PUT`, `LSET`, `RSET`, `WIDTH`, `FILES`, `KILL`, `NAME`, `CHDIR`, `MKDIR`, `RMDIR`, `SHELL`, `ENVIRON`, `COMMAND$`, `INKEY$`, `KEY`, etc.

- Graphics and Sound:

`SCREEN`, `CLS`, `COLOR`, `PSET`, `POINT`, `LINE`, `CIRCLE`, `PAINT`, `DRAW`, `PLAY`, `SOUND`, `BEEP`, `_WIDTH`, `_HEIGHT`, `_PIXELSIZE`, `_RGB`, `_RGB32`, `_RGBA`, `_RGB32A`, `_PALETTECOLOR`, `_LOADIMAGE`, `_PUTIMAGE`, `_FREEIMAGE`, `_NEWIMAGE`, `_COPYIMAGE`, `_MAPTRI`, `_MAPSHOW`, `_MAPFREE`, `_SNDOPEN`, `_SNDPLAY`, `_SNDSTOP`, `_SNDCLOSE`,

`_SNDLEN`, `_SNDPOS`, `_SNDVOL`, `_SNDCOPY`, `_SNDMODULATE`, `_SNDNEW`, `_SNDFREE`, etc.

- String Manipulation:

`+`, `&`, `LEN`, `LEFT$`, `RIGHT$`, `MID$`, `INSTR`, `LTRIM$`, `RTRIM$`, `TRIM$`, `UCASE$`, `LCASE$`, `STR$`, `VAL`, `ASC`, `CHR$`, `STRING$`, `SPACE$`, `FORMAT$`, `HEX$`, `OCT$`, `BIN$`, etc.

- Date and Time:

`DATE$`, `TIME$`, `TIMER`, `DATE`, `TIME`, `NOW`, `DAY`, `MONTH`, `YEAR`, `HOUR`, `MINUTE`, `SECOND`, `WEEKDAY`, `DATEADD`, `DATEDIFF`, `DATEPART`, `DATESERIAL`, `DATEVALUE`, `TIMEVALUE`, `TIMESERIAL`, etc.

- Miscellaneous:

`CONST`, `DEFINT`, `DEFLNG`, `DEFSNG`, `DEFDBL`, `DEFSTR`, `DECLARE`, `FUNCTION`, `END FUNCTION`, `SUB`, `END SUB`, `CALL`, `CALL ABSOLUTE`, `SWAP`, `RANDOMIZE`, `ERASE`, `FRE`, `VARPTR`, `PEEK`, `POKE`, `MEM`, `MEMCOPY`, `MEMFILL`, `MEMFREE`, `OFFSET`, `ERROR`, `ON ERROR`, `RESUME`, `ERR`, `ERL`, `_ERRORLINE`, `SYSTEM`, `END`, `STOP`, etc.

For a complete list of QB64 keywords and functions, and their syntax and usage, please refer to the [QB64 Wiki](https://www.qb64.org/wiki/Category:Keywords).

QB64 Metacommands and Compiler Options

QB64 supports some metacommands and compiler options that

allow you to control the behavior and appearance of your program, such as the title, icon, window size, font, color, sound, graphics, and compatibility. Here is a list of some of the most common and useful QB64 metacommands and compiler options, grouped by category:

- General:

`$CONSOLE`, `$CONSOLE:ONLY`, `$EXEICON`, `$INCLUDE`, `$NOPREFIX`, `$NOSUFFIX`, `$SCREENHIDE`, `$SCREENSHOW`, `$TITLE`, `$TYPELESS`, `$VERSION`, `$WINDOWTITLE`, etc.

- Font and Color:

`$FONT`, `$FONTSIZE`, `$FONTCOLOR`, `$FONTCOLOR:HEX`, `$FONTCOLOR:RGB`, `$FONTCOLOR:RGBA`, `$FONTCOLOR:RGB32`, `$FONTCOLOR:RGB32A`, `$FONTCOLOR:SYSTEM`, `$FONTCOLOR:USER`, `$FONTCOLOR:USER32`, `$FONTCOLOR:USER32A`, `$FONTCOLOR:USERA`, `$FONTCOLOR:USERHEX`, `$FONTCOLOR:USERRGB`, `$FONTCOLOR:USERRGBA`, `$FONTCOLOR:USERRGB32`, `$FONTCOLOR:USERRGB32A`, `$FONTCOLOR:USERX`, `$FONTCOLOR:USERX32`, `$FONTCOLOR:USERX32A`, `$FONTCOLOR:USERXA`, `$FONTCOLOR:USERXHEX`, `$FONTCOLOR:USERXRGB`, `$FONTCOLOR:USERXRGBA`, `$FONTCOLOR:USERXRGB32`, `$FONTCOLOR:USERXRGB32A`, `$FONTCOLOR:X`, `$FONTCOLOR:X32`, `$FONTCOLOR:X32A`, `$FONTCOLOR:XA`, `$FONTCOLOR:XHEX`, `$FONTCOLOR:XRGB`, `$FONTCOLOR:XRGBA`, `$FONTCOLOR:XRGB32`, `$FONTCOLOR:XRGB32A`, `$FONTCOLOR:Z`, `$FONTCOLOR:Z32`, `$FONTCOLOR:Z32A`,

`$FONTCOLOR:ZA`, `$FONTCOLOR:ZHEX`, `
`$FONTCOLOR:ZRGB`, `$FONTCOLOR:ZRGBA`, `
`$FONTCOLOR:ZRGB32`, `$FONTCOLOR:ZRGB32A`, etc.

- Sound:

`$AUDIO`, `$AUDIO:OFF`, `$AUDIO:ON`, `$AUDIO:RATE`, `
`$AUDIO:STEREO`, `$AUDIO:VOLUME`, `$SOUND`, `
`$SOUND:OFF`, `$SOUND:ON`, `$SOUND:RATE`, `
`$SOUND:STEREO`, `$SOUND:VOLUME`, etc.

- Graphics:

`$CHECKING`, `$CHECKING:OFF`, `$CHECKING:ON`, `
`$RESIZE`, `$RESIZE:OFF`, `$RESIZE:ON`, `
`$SCREEN`, `$SCREEN:OFF`, `$SCREEN:ON`, `
`$SCREEN:SIZE`, `$SCREEN:SIZE:FIXED`, `
`$SCREEN:SIZE:MAXIMUM`, `$SCREEN:SIZE:MINIMUM`, `
`$SCREEN:SIZE:RESIZABLE`, `$SCREEN:SIZE:RESTORE`, `
`$SCREEN:SIZE:WINDOW`, `$SCREEN:SIZE:WINDOWED`, `
`$SCREEN:SIZE:WINDOWED:FIXED`, `
`$SCREEN:SIZE:WINDOWED:MAXIMUM`, `
`$SCREEN:SIZE:WINDOWED:MINIMUM`, `
`$SCREEN:SIZE:WINDOWED:RESIZABLE`, `
`$SCREEN:SIZE:WINDOWED:RESTORE`, `
`$SCREEN:SIZE:WINDOWED:WINDOW`, `
`$SCREEN:SIZE:WINDOWED:WINDOW:FIXED`, `
`$SCREEN:SIZE:WINDOWED:WINDOW:MAXIMUM`, `
`$SCREEN:SIZE:WINDOWED:WINDOW:MINIMUM`, `
`$SCREEN:SIZE:WINDOWED:WINDOW:RESIZABLE`, `
`$SCREEN:SIZE:WINDOWED:WINDOW:RESTORE`, `
`$SCREEN:SIZE:WINDOWED:WINDOW:WINDOW`, `
`$SCREEN:SIZE:WINDOWED:WINDOW:WINDOW:FIXED`, `
`$SCREEN:SIZE:WINDOWED:WINDOW:WINDOW:MAXIMUM`, `
`$SCREEN:SIZE:WINDOWED:WINDOW:WINDOW:MINIMUM`, `

```basic
$SCREEN:SIZE:WINDOWED:RESIZABLE 'set the screen size to windowed and resizable

$SCREEN:SIZE:MAXIMUM 'set the screen size to the maximum available

$SCREEN:SIZE:RESTORE 'restore the screen size to the previous value

$SCREEN:SIZE:FIXED 'set the screen size to fixed

$SCREEN:SIZE:MINIMUM 'set the screen size to the minimum allowed

$SCREEN:SIZE:WINDOW 'set the screen size to the window size

$SCREEN:SIZE:WINDOW:FIXED 'set the screen size to the window size and fixed

$SCREEN:SIZE:WINDOW:MAXIMUM 'set the screen size to the window size and maximum

$SCREEN:SIZE:WINDOW:MINIMUM 'set the screen size to the window size and minimum

$SCREEN:SIZE:WINDOW:RESIZABLE 'set the screen size to the window size and resizable

$SCREEN:SIZE:WINDOW:RESTORE 'restore the screen size to the window size and previous value

$SCREEN:SIZE:WINDOW:WINDOW 'set the screen size to the window size and window

$SCREEN:SIZE:WINDOW:WINDOW:FIXED 'set the screen size to the window size and window and fixed

$SCREEN:SIZE:WINDOW:WINDOW:MAXIMUM 'set the screen
```

size to the window size and window and maximum

$SCREEN:SIZE:WINDOW:WINDOW:MINIMUM 'set the screen size to the window size and window and minimum

$SCREEN:SIZE:WINDOW:WINDOW:RESIZABLE 'set the screen size to the window size and window and resizable

$SCREEN:SIZE:WINDOW:WINDOW:RESTORE 'restore the screen size to the window size and window and previous value

` ` `

These are some of the graphics metacommands and compiler options that you can use to control the screen size of your program. You can also use other metacommands and compiler options to control the screen mode, color, font, sound, and compatibility of your program. For a complete list of QB64 metacommands and compiler options, and their syntax and usage, please refer to the [QB64 Wiki](https://www.qb64.org/wiki/Category:Metacommands).

Qb64 Differences And Incompatibilities With Qbasic And Quickbasic

QB64 is mostly compatible with QBasic and QuickBASIC, but there are some differences and incompatibilities that you should be aware of when porting or writing programs. Here is a list of some of the most notable differences and incompatibilities, grouped by category:

- Data Types and Conversion:

QB64 supports some new data types, such as `_BYTE`, `_INTEGER64`, `_FLOAT`, and `_UNSIGNED`, which have different sizes and ranges than the standard data types. QB64 also supports some new conversion functions, such as `CVAR`, `MKI$`, `MKL$`, `MKS$`, `MKD$`, `CVI`, `CVL`, `CVS`, and `CVD`, which can handle different data types and sizes than the standard conversion functions. QB64 also supports some new string formats, such as `HEX$`, `OCT$`, `BIN$`, and `FORMAT $`, which can handle different numeric bases and formats than the standard string formats.

- File and Console Input/Output*:

QB64 supports some new file and console input/output commands and functions, such as `FILES`, `KILL`, `NAME`, `CHDIR`, `MKDIR`, `RMDIR`, `SHELL`, `ENVIRON`, `COMMAND$`, `INKEY$`, and `KEY`, which can handle different file and console operations and parameters than the standard file and console input/output commands and functions. QB64 also supports some new file and console modes and flags, such as `_APPEND`, `_BINARY`, `_INPUT`, `_OUTPUT`, `_RANDOM`, `_SHARED`, `_WINDOWED`, `_CONSOLE`, and `_CONSOLE:ONLY`, which can handle different file and console modes and options than the standard file and console modes and flags.

- Graphics and Sound:

QB64 supports some new graphics and sound commands and functions, such as `_WIDTH`, `_HEIGHT`, `_PIXELSIZE`, `_RGB`, `_RGB32`, `_RGBA`, `_RGB32A`, `_PALETTECOLOR`, `_LOADIMAGE`, `_PUTIMAGE`, `_FREEIMAGE`, `_NEWIMAGE`, `_COPYIMAGE`, `_MAPTRI`, `_MAPSHOW`, `_MAPFREE`, `_SNDOPEN`, `_SNDPLAY`, `_SNDSTOP`, `_SNDCLOSE`, `_SNDLEN`, `_SNDPOS`, `_SNDVOL`, `_SNDCOPY`, `_SNDMODULATE`, `_SNDNEW`, `_SNDFREE`, etc., which can handle different graphics and sound modes, formats, and operations than the standard graphics and sound commands and functions. QB64 also supports some new graphics and sound modes and flags, such as `_NEWIMAGE`,

`_FULLSCREEN`, `_WINDOWED`, `_RESIZABLE`, `_FLIP`, `_MIDDLE`, `_PMODE`, `_COPYPALETTE`, `_BLEND`, `_BLEND_ALPHA`, `_BLEND_ADD`, `_BLEND_SUB`, `_BLEND_MUL`, `_BLEND_DIV`, `_BLEND_INV`, `_BLEND_XOR`, `_BLEND_AND`, `_BLEND_OR`, `_BLEND_NAND`, `_BLEND_NOR`, `_BLEND_EQV`, `_BLEND_IMP`, `_BLEND_NOT`, `_BLEND_ZERO`, `_BLEND_ONE`, `_BLEND_SRC`, `_BLEND_DST`, `_BLEND_SRC_ALPHA`, `_BLEND_DST_ALPHA`, `_BLEND_ONE_MINUS_SRC`, `_BLEND_ONE_MINUS_DST`, `_BLEND_ONE_MINUS_SRC_ALPHA`, `_BLEND_ONE_MINUS_DST_ALPHA`, `_ANIM`, `_ANIM_LOOP`, `_ANIM_PINGPONG`, `_ANIM_REVERSE`, `_ANIM_STOP`, `_ANIM_PLAY`, `_ANIM_PAUSE`, `_ANIM_RESUME`, `_ANIM_SPEED`, `_ANIM_FRAME`, `_ANIM_FRAMES`, `_ANIM_WIDTH`, `_ANIM_HEIGHT`, `_ANIM_X`, `_ANIM_Y`, `_ANIM_ANGLE`, `_ANIM_SCALEX`, `_ANIM_SCALEY`, `_ANIM_COLOR`, `_ANIM_ALPHA`, `_ANIM_LAYER`, `_ANIM_BLEND`, `_ANIM_VISIBLE`, `_ANIM_FLIPX`, `_ANIM_FLIPY`, `_ANIM_ROTATE`, `_ANIM_SCALE`, `_ANIM_MOVE`, `_ANIM_DRAW`, `_ANIM_FREE`, etc., which can handle different graphics and sound modes and options than the standard graphics and sound modes and flags.

- String Manipulation:

QB64 supports some new string manipulation commands and functions, such as `&`, `LTRIM$`, `RTRIM$`, `TRIM$`, `UCASE$`, `LCASE$`, `STRING$`, `SPACE$`, `HEX$`, `OCT$`, `BIN$`, and `FORMAT$`, which can handle different string operations and formats than the standard string manipulation commands and functions.

- Date and Time:

QB64 supports some new date and time commands and

functions, such as `DATE`, `TIME`, `NOW`, `DAY`, `MONTH`, `YEAR`, `HOUR`, `MINUTE`, `SECOND`, `WEEKDAY`, `DATEADD`, `DATEDIFF`, `DATEPART`, `DATESERIAL`, `DATEVALUE`, `TIMEVALUE`, `TIMESERIAL`, etc., which can handle different date and time operations and formats than the standard date and time commands and functions.

- Miscellaneous:

QB64 supports some new miscellaneous commands and functions, such as `MEM`, `MEMCOPY`, `MEMFILL`, `MEMFREE`, `OFFSET`, `ERROR`, `ON ERROR`, `RESUME`, `_ERRORLINE`, `SYSTEM`, `STOP`, etc., which can handle different miscellaneous operations and parameters than the standard miscellaneous commands and functions.

For a complete list of QB64 differences and incompatibilities with QBasic and QuickBASIC, and their explanations and solutions, please refer to the [QB64 Wiki](https://www.qb64.org/wiki/QB64_Differences_from_QBASIC).

Qb64 Resources And Community Links

QB64 is a vibrant and active project that has a lot of resources and community links that you can use to learn more about the language, get help and support, share your programs and ideas, and contribute to the development and improvement of QB64. Here is a list of some of the most useful and popular QB64 resources and community links, grouped by category:

- Official Website: The official website of QB64, where you can download the latest version of QB64, access the online documentation and wiki, browse the online forum and chat, and donate to the project. The website is: https://www.qb64.org/

- Online Documentation and Wiki**: The online documentation and wiki of QB64, where you can find detailed information and examples on QB64 keywords and functions, metacommands and compiler options, differences and incompatibilities with QBasic and QuickBASIC, libraries and extensions, and more. The documentation and wiki are: https://www.qb64.org/wiki/Main_Page

- Online Forum and Chat: The online forum and chat of QB64, where you can interact with other QB64 users and developers, ask questions and get answers, share your programs and feedback, report bugs and issues, suggest features and improvements, and more. The forum and chat are: https://www.qb64.org/forum/ and https://www.qb64.org/portal/chat/

- Online IDE and Compiler: The online IDE and compiler of QB64, where you can write and run QB64 code in your web browser, without installing anything on your computer. You can also save and load your code, share your code with others, and export your code to HTML5. The online IDE and compiler are: https://www.qb64.org/portal/ide/ and https://www.qb64.org/portal/compiler/

Qbjs: Deploying Your Qb64 Program To The Web

QBjs is a tool that allows you to deploy your QB64 program to the web, by converting your QB64 code to JavaScript and HTML5. You can use QBjs to create web applications and games with QB64, and share them with others online. QBjs supports most of the QB64 features and libraries, such as graphics, sound, input, GX, and InForm. QBjs also supports some web-specific features, such as web storage, web sockets, web workers, and web assembly.

To use QBjs, you need to download and install the QBjs tool from the [QB64 website](https://www.qb64.org/portal/qbjs/). You also need to have a web server to host your web application or game. You can use any web server that supports PHP, such as Apache, Nginx, or IIS. You can also use a local web server, such as XAMPP, WAMP, or MAMP, for testing and debugging purposes.

To deploy your QB64 program to the web with QBjs, you need to follow these steps:

1. Write your QB64 program in the QB64 IDE, and save it as a `.bas` file. You can also use any text editor to write your QB64 code, as long as you save it as a `.bas` file.

2. Run the QBjs tool, and select your `.bas` file as the input file. You can also specify some options for the output file, such as the title, icon, size, and quality of the web application or game.

3. Click the "Convert" button, and wait for the conversion process to finish. The QBjs tool will generate a `.html` file and a `.js` file, as well as some other files and folders, depending on the features and libraries used by your QB64 program.

4. Copy the generated files and folders to your web server, and make sure they have the correct permissions and paths. You can also edit the `.html` file and the `.js` file, if you want to customize or optimize your web application or game.

5. Open the `.html` file in your web browser, and enjoy your web application or game. You can also share the URL of the `.html` file with others, so they can access your web application or game online.